Amanda and Her Mother
Enter Into "Lifetime of Treatment!"

Written by Jim Rauth
Illustrated by Mark Morel and Jim Rauth

This book is dedicated to anyone who has an addiction or knows someone who has. Our culture is on a quick road to nowhere if we choose not to live moment to moment in reality,

Jim Rauth

Note to caregivers: This book is designed to be read from caregiver to child. Any time you see a section in parentheses (Ex: Caregiver...this where you pause to see if the child has questions, thoughts or insights). Educate and enjoy!

Amanda's mommy, Jane was walking on crutches as
she entered the kitchen to have a glass of milk.

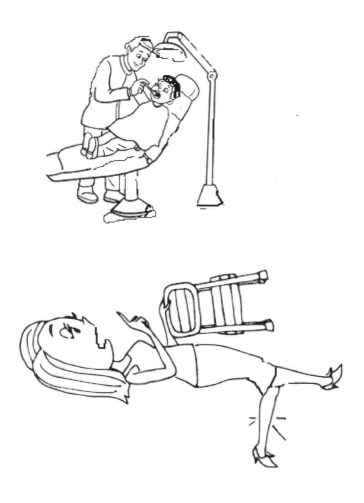

Jane had hurt her foot at work in the dentist office, she was carrying step stool and she accidentally tripped.

Jane twisted her ankle very badly and the ambulance
came to take her to the hospital.

When Amanda found out about her mom being hurt,
she was very frightened and upset.

Doctor Randy wrapped Jane's ankle at the hospital, but she was still in a lot of pain. So he gave her a pill called a pain killer to help the pain go away.

When Jane first hurt her foot, she slept all night and
most of the day, too!

Amanda was very mad because when she would arrive
home from school, she and her mom would play a game
outside called "hopscotch,"
But her mother couldn't play anymore!

But as the days went by, Amanda started to invite over
her two best friends in the world,
Ella and Natalie, along with her new friend, Carla, who
just moved into the neighborhood.
Amanda taught them how to play hopscotch.

Natalie said, "Look! I can jump high!
I'm going to be in the Olympics!"

It was Ella's turn and she said,
"Look, I'm going to be in the Olympics too."
And she was being silly and did a somersault.

Natalie yelled, "It's your turn Carla!"
And Carla yelled,
"You're the best new friends anyone could have!"
And then she jumped on the number 1 square.

Day after day, Jane's foot still hurt, so she took more and more pain killers to try to make the pain go away.

After several weeks, Jane began to walk again.
But even though her ankle was better, she kept taking
the pain killers because
Jane thought they made her feel happy.

As time went on, Jane continued taking the pain killers and they did not make her think she was happy any more.

While Jane was at home, Amanda went to school and, instead of listening to her teacher, she would think and worry about her mom. She was also mad at her mother for taking pills because they didn't play hopscotch anymore.

Then one day, when Amanda was on her way home
from school, the ambulance was outside her house.
They were taking her mommy to the treatment center
because she took too many pain killers and they made
Jane feel very dizzy. Amanda was so frightened.

Amanda and her grandmother went to see her mom at the treatment center, but she was sleeping. Amanda was very, very worried. Jane slept the whole night and the whole next day.

Amanda asks,
"Do you know what a treatment center is?"

(Caregiver: It's like a hospital and a school, they help
people get physically better and they teach the patients
like Jane how to stay healthy without the pain killers)

The next day, Jane woke up and the doctors said that she needed to stay at the treatment center for a whole month. Amanda's grandma and grandpa were there too.

Amanda's mom's counselor, Megan, who works at the
treatment center, explained to her that her mother has
a disease called addiction. Megan asked Amanda how
she felt about her Mom staying at the treatment center
for a whole month. Amanda said she felt okay about it,
but she really didn't.

Amanda asks,
"Do you know what an addiction is?"

(Caregiver: An addiction, for the person that has it, is a disease that drives the person to keep doing an activity over and over, even though it may not be good for them. Kind of like taking too many pills or eating too much. Their brains forget their "off" switch. It's like a broken arm that doesn't work right until it has time to heal.)

While Amanda's mommy was at the treatment center, day after day, Amanda kept staying with grandma and grandpa on their farm. Amanda went to school and when she came home, she fed the chickens. It helped her not think about her mom being away.

But some evenings Amanda went to her room to cry because she missed her mom. She was also angry with her mother for not being with her. And she was confused as to why her mom had to have this disease. During this time, Amanda would also wonder where her dad was living, but it was mostly about her mom because she was used to her mom taking care of her.

At school Amanda's teacher Ms. Johnson asked, "How are things going at home?" Amanda put on a great big smile and responded, "Great!" even though she was very sad on the inside.
But Ms. Johnson knew that Amanda missed her mom and that she was very, very sad and upset.

So Ms. Johnson made an appointment for Amanda to see Mr. Mike, the school psychologist. Mr. Mike doesn't fix runny noses or broken arms, but he helps people who are sad, angry, upset or confused. Just like Amanda was about the situation with her mom.

Amanda started to tell Mr. Mike that she was upset because Samantha's mom was in treatment for an addiction too. Amanda wondered why her mother picks her up after school.

Mr. Mike explained, "Samantha's mom is in day treatment." And that her mom, Jane, would have to be in day treatment after she is released from the treatment center. So while Amanda is in school, her mom will still be getting help.

Amanda asks,
"Do you know what day treatment is?"

(Caregiver: Day treatment is when a person goes for help for their addiction in the afternoons. Amanda's mom will always be in recovery, which means that through her whole life she will be getting help. She will be going to an hour meeting for help at least twice a week for the rest of her life.)

Mr. Mike also asked Amanda how she felt about her
Mom being in treatment for her whole life.

Amanda asks
"Should I tell Mr. Mike the truth and tell him I that feel sad about my mom being treatment or should I tell him what I told Ms. Johnson that I feel great?"

(Caregiver: Mr. Mike is trying to help Amanda, but she has to open up so he can help.)

"That's right! I should tell Mr. Mike how I truly feel - that I'm sad. He might be able to help me feel better."

"Now my mom and I are home together and my mom has to go to meeting with other people like her. She goes to meetings twice a week. The meetings make mom feel better, and if my mom feels better, I do too."

"I'm so happy that my mom is back home with me. Now I don't cry so much anymore - just once in a while, when I scrape my knee or hurt my elbow. But now that my mom and her disease of addiction are better, I just mostly dance!"

"I still see Mr. Mike once a month and we talk about what I'm happy about or sometimes things that are bothering me. I also go to meetings with other children that have Moms or Dads that have the disease of addiction just like I do. Mom and I are doing great, we just do life one day at a time!"

Made in the USA
Middletown, DE
11 September 2024

60162244R00022